D1076270

Published by the Penguin Group
Penguin Books Ltd, 80 Strand, London WC2R 0RL, England
Penguin Group (USA) Inc., 375 Hudson Street, New York, New York 10014, USA
Penguin Group (Canada), 90 Eglinton Avenue East, Suite 700, Toronto, Ontario,
Canada M4P 2Y3 (a division of Pearson Penguin Canada Inc.)
Penguin Ireland, 25 St Stephen's Green, Dublin 2, Ireland
(a division of Penguin Books Ltd)
Penguin Group (Australia), 250 Camberwell Road, Camberwell, Victoria 3124,
Australia (a division of Pearson Australia Group Pty Ltd)
Penguin Books India Pvt Ltd, 11 Community Centre, Panchsheel Park,
New Delhi – 110 017, India
Penguin Group (NZ), 67 Apollo Drive, Rosedale, North Shore 0632,
New Zealand (a division of Pearson New Zealand Ltd)
Penguin Books (South Africa) (Pty) Ltd, 24 Sturdee Avenue, Rosebank,
Johannesburg 2196, South Africa

Penguin Books Ltd, Registered Offices:
80 Strand, London WC2R 0RL, England
www.penguin.com

First published 2009
1
Copyright © Take That, 2009
The moral right of the authors has been asserted
For further permissions see pages 206-207

All rights reserved
Without limiting the rights under copyright reserved above, no part of this
publication may be reproduced, stored in or introduced into a retrieval
system, or transmitted, in any form or by any means (electronic, mechanical,
photocopying, recording or otherwise), without the prior written permission
of both the copyright owner and the above publisher of this book

Printed and bound by Firmengruppe APPL, aprinta druck, Wemding, Germany
Colour reproduction by Altaimage
A CIP catalogue record for this book is available from the British Library
ISBN: 978-0-718-15578-0

Where directional symbols appear throughout this book, reference is being
made to a spread that either precedes or succeeds the text depending on
the direction of the arrow

www.greenpenguin.co.uk

Penguin Books is committed to a sustainable future
for our business, our readers and our planet.
The book in your hands is made from paper
certified by the Forest Stewardship Council.

TAKE THAT / TAKE ONE

Llyfrgelloedd Sir Gaerfyrddin
Dyd......................
Ffôn....................
County borough Libraries

We'd all literally clamber to be the centre of attention on camera. We'd fight to get in shot.

MARK —————— There were two places that always went down best on our very early club tours. One was Newcastle and the other was Hollywood in Romford. Whenever we turned up there was absolute chaos.

JASON —————— It was always one of our favourites on the club circuit. We had a little following that we'd built up from under-18s discos, gay clubs and schools. Word had got round about us. As soon as we saw it on the itinerary we were all made up. Those Essex girls got a really bad name around that time, but they looked dead fit to us. They seemed prettier somehow. We actually used to say Essex girls only got a bad name because everyone was jealous of them because they were all really fit.

GARL _____ A guy named Will Smack shot the video for 'Promises'
after a show at Hollywood. We were very big there.
The guy that ran the place was really very nice. Romford
was a good place for us if we needed someone from the
record company or a magazine to come down and see us
because it was so easy to get to from London. I don't
think I'd go back to the bleached hair again. The biggest
pain was the bloody nuisance of maintaining it every
three weeks. Once the roots came in. That was it…

HOWARD _____ What always happened in Hollywood was that the women would be downstairs going mental at us, but all their boyfriends would be up on the balcony spitting on us.

HOWARD —————————— I've given almost all the stuff I've worn on stage through the years away, but the 'Do What You Like' codpiece and leather jacket I've kept, for some reason. Me and Jason bought the jackets from Kensington Market and they weren't cheap! Two hundred quid a pop! We were doing what we were told to do at the time, wearing what we were told to wear, and we didn't even think of questioning it. Everyone's jackets would come off a minute into the routine, though Rob wasn't keen to take his off because he was wearing a tasty all-in-one ski suit underneath. We loved it, though. We knew that we were on our way. The littlest things meant such a lot to us, even down to getting free catering on the set.

JASON —————————— We'd all literally clamber to be centre of attention on camera. We'd fight to get in shot. We'd only been in development for six months before we filmed the 'Do What You Like' video. I had my hair darkened for it at Pierre Alexander in Manchester, which was Nigel, our manager's hairdresser's. Nigel had found me dancing on *The Hitman and Her* and when I was dancing my hair got darker from all the sweat. He liked it. So I got it done for the video, with a little piece added at the front so it flopped over my face on photo shoots. The 'Do What You Like' outfits are iconic now. Nigel really knew what he was doing.

We all felt ridiculous, of course. Gary felt the most ridiculous. But we'd lose any self-consciousness because it was our little gang. We were comrades straight off. Howard and myself would always take cues off each other, Mark thought everything was mega and Robbie was a bit like a little brother to us. Gary just didn't get the outfits, though.

GARY   All the songs I was coming in with for the band at first were like bad Stock, Aitken and Waterman rip-offs and none of the boys wanted to sound like Kylie Minogue. They wanted to sound like New Kids On The Block. 'Do What You Like' was my attempt to write us a 'Hanging Tough'. They wanted something cool, and I thought, 'how am I going to do this? I don't even know any cool words.' So I was shipped off to see the songwriter Ray Hedges who had written a big hit. I went to his studio in Surrey and he had this beat going and a piano riff, which sounded like a lot of the house music that was around at the time and we wrote 'Do What You Like' over it.

If someone asks you to go and write a single now you'd maybe do two or three co-writes and have a selection to pick from. But so often at the start with Take That I'd write one song, everyone would say, 'that'll do' and we'd be making a video for it three weeks later. It's impossible to tell what we'd be doing three years later here, let alone now. How the hell did we get away with that gear?

JASON —————— We did a really strong routine to 'Apache' on the first arena tour. It was us working out what we could do as a band, and those parts of the show were brilliant for me. Robbie would do a rap, Howard was the human beat box, Gary was wearing some big outrageous Elton John outfit. We were young and fit, and I felt really strong and powerful as a dancer. We'd found where we were going and found ways to work that weren't the same as a normal, conventional boy band.

MARK —————— It was a real honour for me to be dancing with Jason, he choreographed the routine and, believe me, it was way beyond my natural capabilities. He was patient though, and I got there in the end. We rocked! The hat must have been thrown on stage by somebody in the audience…

GARY _____ Every tour we'd do an off-the-wall section, something a bit mad. All five of us would go down to my studio and make a track out of a breakbeat so that we could feature everyone's best bits individually. Of course I always wanted to be Elton John. He's always been a big hero of mine. He came to see us at a show in Wembley with Paula Yates and invited us all to dinner at his house the following night. It was one of the few times Nigel let us meet someone like that. Often very famous people would come to our shows and we'd never even know about it until afterwards. Going for dinner at Elton's house was just the biggest eye-opener for us all. Of how enormous he was. We thought we were so big at the time but you'd see all his platinum discs on his wall and it was humbling to realize we'd only just started, really.

When we got there Nigel muttered to me, 'I can't believe that John Reid's here.' Other artists were a bit of a no-no. But other managers in the same room as his band? That was major. The two of them got on really well in the end. They probably had a bit of a moan at each other about their artists. It was actually a really, really lovely night, certainly one I've never forgotten.

JASON ——————— Gus Douglas was our first tour manager, hence the name 'Gus' on the back wall. I'm sure he hated us. He was a really eccentric old rocker, tall and skinny with a ponytail. He used to stand at the side of the stage, bawling at us: 'Hurry up, you tap-dancers!' or 'Come on, you Northern monkeys, I want to go home!' There was a part of his heart that he kept for us, but he wasn't very good at showing it. I've not seen him since. We've invited him to a few of the comeback gigs and he's never taken us up on the offer. Maybe he still hates us!

DRESSING
ROOM

← BAND

GUS
MANAGEMENT
←

SHOWER →

PRODUCTION
←

TOILETS
→

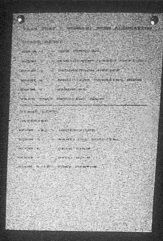

TAKE
THAT

MARK —————————— We were never afraid of taking our clothes off. But the funny thing about Take That back in the 90s was that we seemed to become more popular with the more clothes we actually put on. It was a change for the good. We were more popular once we'd toned down the codpieces, the leather and the naked chests. The leather and lycra had all been put to bed by the time of the 'It Only Takes a Minute' video, very early on. What didn't go until much later were the hefty boots. We called them clodhoppers. They were murder to dance in. And they followed us everywhere.

GARY —————— We shot the 'Relight My Fire' video at Ministry of Sound. Nigel was the only one at this time who was getting out and rubbing shoulders with real life. We just worked all the time. He kept talking about this song that he'd heard at the end of nightclubs called 'Relight My Fire' and I didn't really like it much. But he said everyone went mad for it in the clubs, and he was right. Then he came up with the idea of bringing in Lulu and I thought, 'Well, my mum'll like that.' 'Relight' was earmarked as Robbie's song first. We did our backing vocals and then Lulu came in and did her bit, which turned out to be a real eye-opener. She'd drink water with ginger and lemon before she sang and it was so cool to see what a professional singer did because I really had no idea.

I used to just go in and sing straight off, and she was a bit horrified that I didn't do a proper warm-up. Robbie was in the studio for two days, trying to get a handle on the lead vocal, and his brain was exploding. He just couldn't nail it. On the last day Nigel called me and asked if I could try singing the lead. It was the perfect key for me. I sang it twice and got a call the following Monday morning from him saying, 'This is it. It's the next single and it's going to be a number one.' It was a pivotal moment for Robbie and the band. He didn't have a song on the album at that point and I feel like that was the start of his rebellion. It knocked his confidence, so to try and make up for it, I shot off to Eliot Kennedy's studio in Sheffield and wrote 'Everything Changes' for him to make sure he had a vocal on the record.

The performing of the songs never bothered me; it was the writing I didn't like anyone else getting involved in. Rob was always trying to prove himself to Nigel. He'd been swept aside again and it must have hurt.

MARK —————— It wasn't my idea to cut off my T-shirt at the midriff
▢▢ for the 'Relight My Fire' video. But I could've said
→ no. The cut-off crop top is one of my worst fashion mistakes ever, but I quite like how controversial the T-shirt was. They used to blur out the druggy message on the front of it on *The Chart Show* and MTV, but I didn't even know what it meant at the time. I still thought it said Johnson's Baby Powder until three years later. The casting for the video was done in real clubs the weekend before. All the clubbers were great. It felt real. You can get into a bubble as a band and it wasn't often that we got to mix with other people.

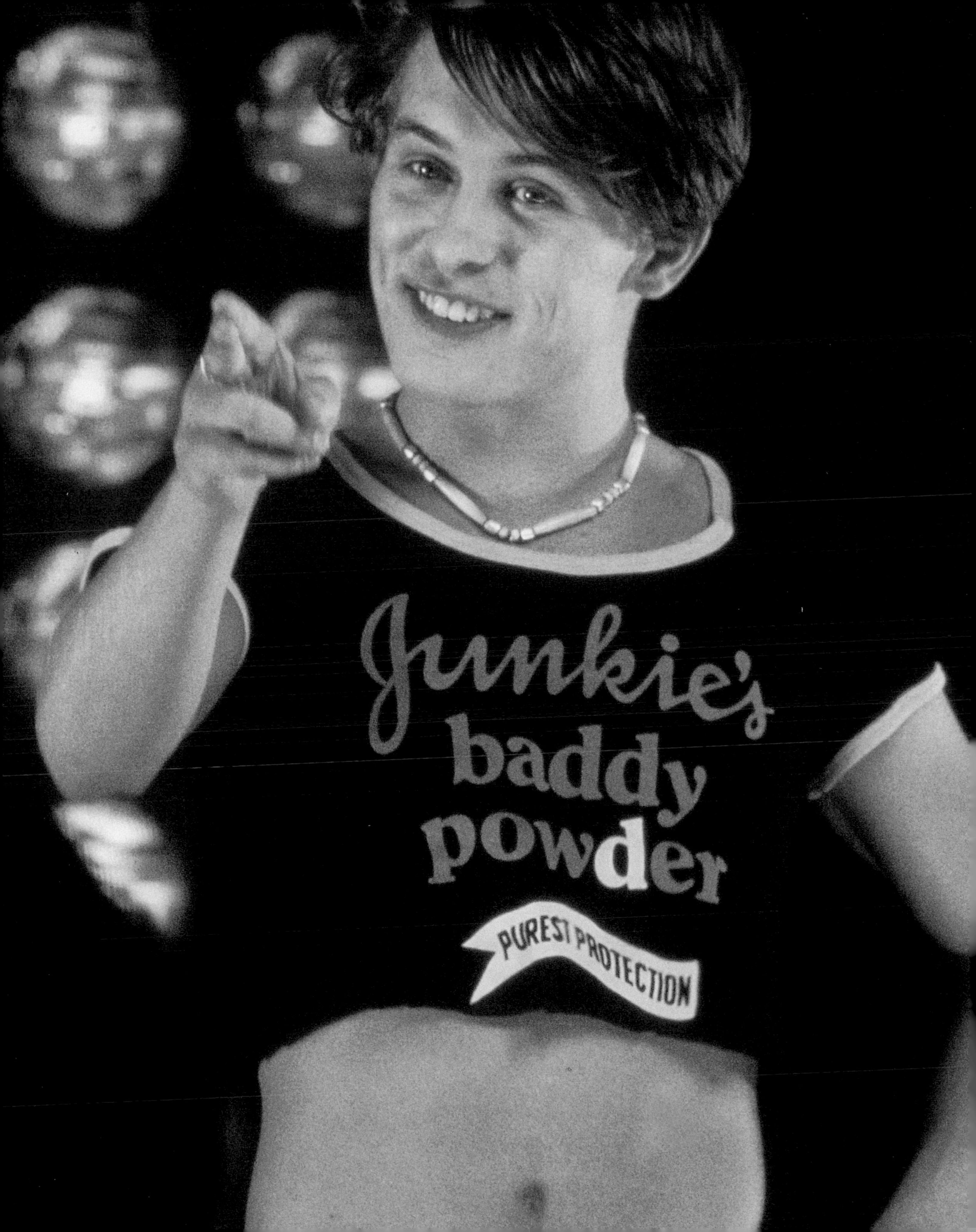
Junkie's
baddy
powder
PUREST PROTECTION

HOWARD ———————— It was Kim Gavin's idea for us to do the Beatles medley and he staged it brilliantly. It felt like a real moment for us and it went down a storm.

MARK ——————— The first time we went to the *Brit Awards* was the first time that I'd ever worn a tuxedo. We were completely star-struck that evening.

HOWARD ——————— The whole night was just us jumping in front of other bands and grabbing a photo with them. We were more like fans than artists. Tori Amos was lovely, so was George Michael. They must've wondered what the hell we were doing. The pop acts were all stuck on the *Smash Hits* road show back then and we never felt we were supposed to be at the *Brits*. We were the cheesy pop group and they were the credible artists. There was a very clear distinction between the two things.

MARK _____ I loved the concept behind the 'Babe' video, of the soldier returning home from war. It was my first attempt at acting. I used to fancy the pants off the girl in the video – Rachel Buckley. She worked at Nigel's agency in Manchester. I had quite a big crush on her, so I was very happy with the casting. I like the song but it was very much me then, not so much now. I got a Christmas card off the little boy who was playing my son for years afterwards. He'll be in his late teens now and I guess a little embarrassed about the whole thing.

HOWARD ——————— 'Babe' is married to Mark as a song. It's still very popular with the fans. He should be very proud of it.

MARK ——————— 'Babe' was my first lead vocal. I had real mixed feelings about it. I was so nervous during the whole recording process. I must have sung it at least twenty-five times. I can still remember Gaz calling to say 'Mark, I've got a song for you.' I used to practise it all the time in the car, which was how I learned all the Take That songs. Gary would give us his demos on a tape; I'd fill up the Volkswagen Golf and away we'd go.

MARK —————— I love this picture, I'm guessing we're in Germany, it always seemed to be cold and snowing every time we went there. I think Jason looks fantastic here, like a star. He probably went along the whole line and signed something for everyone. I like to think we've always had a great relationship with our audience.

MARK ——————— I did two versions of 'Babe' on *Top of the Pops* that day, on different stages to make it feel like it had been recorded at different times. The second one was in case we got the Christmas number one with it. But Mr Blobby beat us to it. There's a hidden version of it out there somewhere.

JASON ——————— 'Babe' was our fourth number one and the first Take That song I ever learnt the chords for on the guitar. I was playing it on the beach in Miami once and a girl came up to me and said 'Oh my gawd! That's such a pretty song' and I didn't have the heart to tell her I hadn't written it. It makes me a bit sad to think that *Top of the Pops* has gone now. What's wrong with us that we couldn't hold that together? It just went, and there didn't even seem to be that much fuss.

HOWARD ——————— I always used to say in interviews that I fancied Cindy Crawford and everything you said like that was picked up on by the fans. So one of them had made this cut-out of the two of us together. I was a big fan of Seabrook's crinkle-cut salt and vinegar crisps at the time, too, and the company were so made up I mentioned them they sent me a massive, industrial-sized box of their crisps. I never did get to meet Cindy Crawford though.

MARK ——————— We were a proud bunch. There was never a moment, ever, where we didn't give everything to our performance. The concentration was intense. Gary was holding the band together. There are these two big, physical men behind him and me, with Rob to the side. It's a proud moment on stage for all of us.

JASON ——————— It was a Take That tradition first time round to finish the show off in white outfits. These stages seemed so massive at the time, but compared to what we've just done it looks quite small, almost like a little Lego set.

HOWARD ——————— There was a happiness to the end of each concert. I sometimes wonder how we managed to do three shows night after night. There was such an energy to it. And we would give it our all for the entire length of the show. Absolutely 100 per cent.

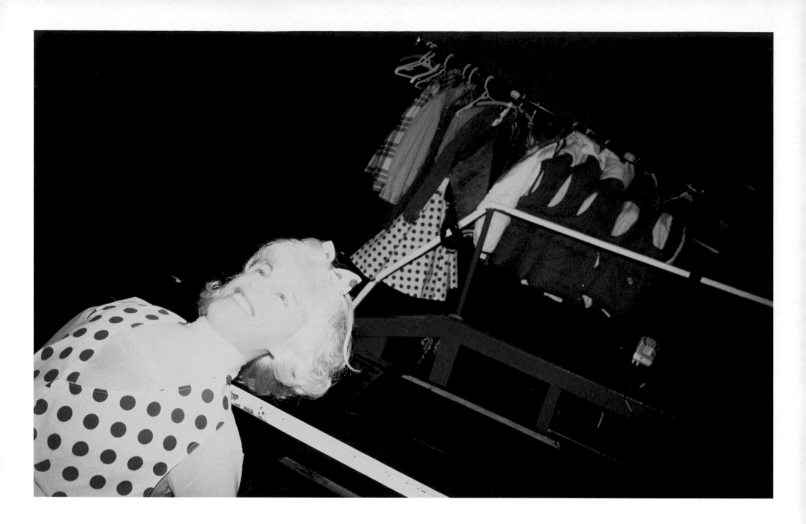

JASON ——————— It was the best time for all of us. Right in the middle of the performance. When you're on stage you all feel at your best. It can be a bit out of body. It's indescribable, really. The dummy of me that Howard danced with in the 'Grease' medley on our first arena tour looked eerily similar to me. I'll be honest, there was something a little bit freaky about that dummy.

MARK ——————— Cheeky. Sweet. Young. It was always a lot of fun with Rob. You need your partner in crime in a band and for me that was Rob. There was cockiness to it all but there was a sincerity, too.

GARY ——————— Mark will never say this. A girl has never broken his heart. But Robbie did the day he left the band. He was inconsolable. They really were like brothers.

JASON ——————— We always loved doing *San Remo* in Italy. It was the TV show to do there and you'd get instant returns on it. Even more so than with *Top of the Pops*. Italy and Germany have always been great territories for us with really passionate audiences. The gesticulation and affection always seemed multiplied from everywhere else.

JASON ———————— Howard taught me how to do a backflip. When I was a break-dancer I could never do it. I didn't have the bottle. There is a little bit of technique involved but it's mainly nerve. We'd always get the backflip in early doors on the tours, so we did it to the second song, 'Promises', on this one. It couldn't be further away from the earlier performance at Hollywood in Romford, really.

GARY ———————— We'd always open the show with two or three up-tempo songs to try and win the audience over. We'd hit it really hard on the first three songs to get the energy right up and they were with us from the off.

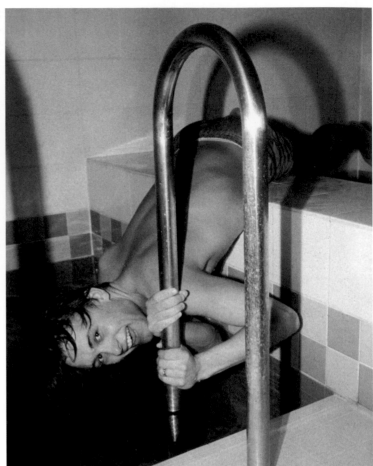

GARY —————— Robbie was such an important figure in Take That
stage one. This is just typical Rob. He had his head
shaved to a number one crop because we'd just
gone to number one with 'Relight My Fire'. He was
beginning to realize his power. He used to remind
us quite regularly how he was making the band cool
and giving it a bit of edge. It never went unnoticed
by Rob. But the funny thing was, he was right.

HOWARD —————— There was a kind of on-stage flirtation that would
happen most nights with Robbie. It was part
of what made him and what still makes him a
fantastic performer.

HOWARD —————————— Nobody was allowed in Mark's hotel room on the tour Lulu did with us. He'd hide himself away and light his joss sticks and meditate. That was what he told us, anyway. Lulu definitely had an influence on him.

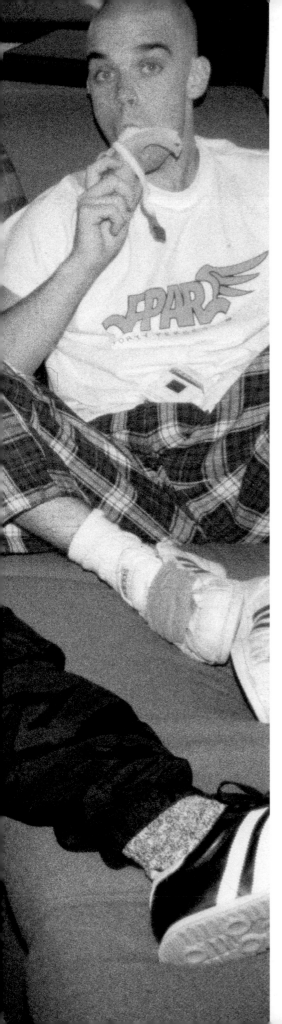

JASON ———————— Of course towards the end Rob became a bit of a dissident and didn't want to be a part of us but there were a lot of moments like this where the synchronicity was just right with him. I loved my Adidas Sambas. Those trainers were significant. When I was a kid growing up in Manchester there were Adidas Mamba, Bamba and Samba. Mamba were the cheapest and so of course they were the ones I had to have. Samba were the most expensive. The kids at school with Samba were the top boys. They were £12.99 a pair. Wearing a pair of Adidas Samba was a symbol of making it for me.

MARK ———————— God knows why the gay rumours started…

GARY —————— There was always, and there still is always, a lot of laughter around the band. It's at the heart of what being in Take That's about. It comes down to how much we enjoy being with each other. We still play pile-on now.

MARK —————— Pile-on was a game that we'd always play. It was usually Gary at the bottom. We still play it now.

JASON —————— There's a very happy energy around Take That. Robbie always instigated the pile-on situation. It's brotherly. We could be five years old when we're playing it, and we still do it now. Gary was always a little bit detached from it. He always had his own ideas. He did feel different from us from the start, but the longer it went on the more of a laugh he had with us. There's no sense of Nigel in Gary's ear here, telling him he's the golden ticket. Myself, Howard and Mark always felt akin to each other. Rob and Gary were always just a little bit different. But at times like this everything was pure and happy.

HOWARD —————— Pile-on is a Take That tradition that lives to this day. It's daft and it makes you laugh. What more do you want out of a game?

MARK ——————— Every day in Take That the first time round there was an itinerary, but the itineraries in Asia would be detailed to the last second. With someone as impulsive as Rob it could be a recipe for absolute chaos. Jet lag when travelling from one country to another was always a bit of a bummer and travelling from England to America to Asia was about as hard as it could get. I can remember we used to fall asleep in interviews; we'd be dropping like flies.

MARK —————— This picture was taken during our 'Everything Changes Tour'. It was the longest tour we had done. I remember being absolutely knackered by the end of it.

GARY —————— Jess was my first dog, a rescue Alsatian. I got her when she was six months old and had her until she was ten. She went everywhere with me. She came on tour with us and Philip snapped us together back stage at the GMEX in Manchester. She's the only dog I've ever had that I didn't have to have put down. I loved her.

HOWARD —————— We stayed in Stanbridge in someone's house to rehearse and Gary brought his dog, Jess, along with him. She had an incident in a greenhouse at rehearsals. Jess legged it through the glass and split her face up. It was very upsetting. I had a girlfriend then who I had to keep quiet about, which was very difficult for me. She would've never been allowed to come to Stanbridge.

HOWARD —————— I always shaved my chest in the early days. That's changed now. But the nipple ring remains. The chain was given to me by a fan and I'd wear it all the time. The first time you were sent stuff was unbelievable. A fan gave me a present that had belonged to her grandma, who'd died. I sent it back to her saying she'd regret it later. Mark was the first person to get a fan letter. We were all renting a house on Heaton Moor Road in Stockport and a letter came through the door for Mark. We couldn't believe it. We were all dead jealous. We only lasted a week in the house because there weren't enough beds for us. One of us had to kip on the couch. Gary probably had a four-poster bed, mind. With his own butler…

JASON _____ It's the happiness that gets you every time with the fans.

HOWARD —————— 'Sure' is one of the only routines I got sick of.
The video wasn't very good, either. We were very
obviously following the trends of the time. All the
R&B videos from that period had people at house
parties and they'd all collapse at the end. So we had
a video with a house party where we all collapsed at
the end. It was absolutely shite, to be honest.

HOWARD ——————— I was finding my own identity, and getting my eyebrow pierced and having the dreadlocks were just a part of that. The idea for the dreadlocks came from one of the stylists at a hairdresser's in Manchester called Antennae. There was no point trying to grow dreads because it would've taken years and turned out a bit manky, so I had a spiral perm and then backcombed it and let it settle down, which was exactly what she'd told me to do. Much as I loved it at the time, I couldn't have been more relieved when I took them out years later. As soon as they were cut out it felt fresh and I began to feel confident about myself again. If you look very closely you'll see the bloke doing my piercing has got a Take That sign on his arm. Or something very close to it…

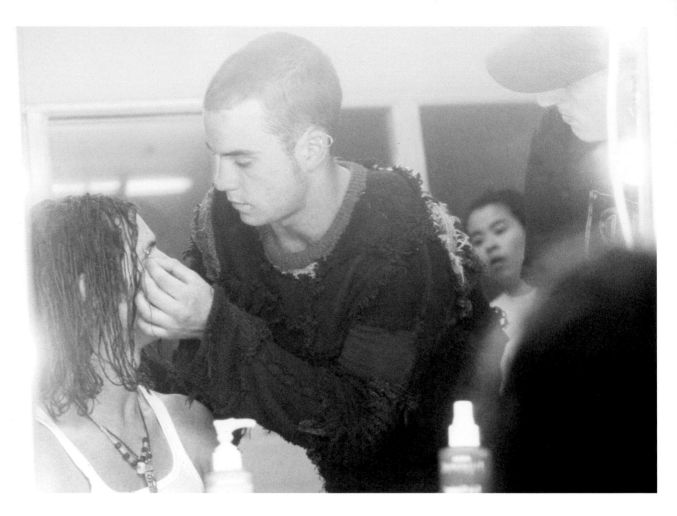

JASON —————— Howard was Rob's favourite, after Mark. He looked up to Howard like you would a big brother. Me and Howard had left school and had jobs by the time it all started with Take That, but Robbie hadn't. Those little things mean a lot when you're sixteen years old.

MARK _____ At the side of the arena in Milan there were loads of basketball courts. We were so fit back then it was unbelievable. We'd play football or basketball for two hours and then go on to do a show. We had so much energy.

GARY — We loved Diana. She'd booked a headline band for her charity show at Wembley and they let her down so she called us a week before and booked us to play. We went to Kensington Palace the day before the show to meet her, so we knew her a little bit. The Christmas afterwards she sent us all hand-written cards. Mine was one of the few things I packed to take with me when I left home for the first time to move into my house.

JASON — We were at Kensington Palace for about two hours and she was lovely. Nigel was with us at the palace but when he was with us I never really felt like I could let go. He did most of the talking with her and I'm sure if he hadn't been there we would've all flapped a bit. We talked a lot about the press. She said what a hard time she was getting from the paparazzi and Nigel said, 'Oh, my boys get it all the time.' We'd already been to Elton John's house by this time and had dinner there, and I must say that he did have a bigger palace.

MARK — The famous story about meeting Diana was Jason's shirt. He'd worn the same one to Kensington Palace the day before, and she made a joke about him being the scruffy one. Which he loved. You didn't feel unworthy in Diana's presence. There was a real compassion about her.

HOWARD — She was a beautiful lady. I drank orange cordial at Kensington Palace because I was too scared to ask for a cuppa. I've still got the Christmas card that Princess Diana sent to me that year.

JASON ——————— I used to carry around nuts and seeds and rye bread everywhere in Tupperware. We were all a bit concerned about what we ate to keep the energy up, but I think I went a bit over the top. I was reading a fan letter. Mark always got the most fan mail, then Rob as he came up through the ranks, then Gary and Howard and me. We all wanted the most. Of course we did.

HOWARD ——————— The irony is that Robbie owned a flat just opposite this hotel, after he left the band. He hadn't moved in there at this time. Jay was forever eating his nuts and seeds and I was busy falling out with Gary. We knew it was over. I argued with Gary and felt like throwing the whole thing in there and then.

MARK —————— We were a very close and affectionate band at
this time. There was a lot of hugging and kissing,
I personally never used tongues.

GARY —————— A fan had won a radio competition to meet us in Germany and she brought along a huge collection of memorabilia that included her bra. This was her entire collection. She'd made little posters of us all and she had some manuscripts for the songs. And her bra. Obviously.

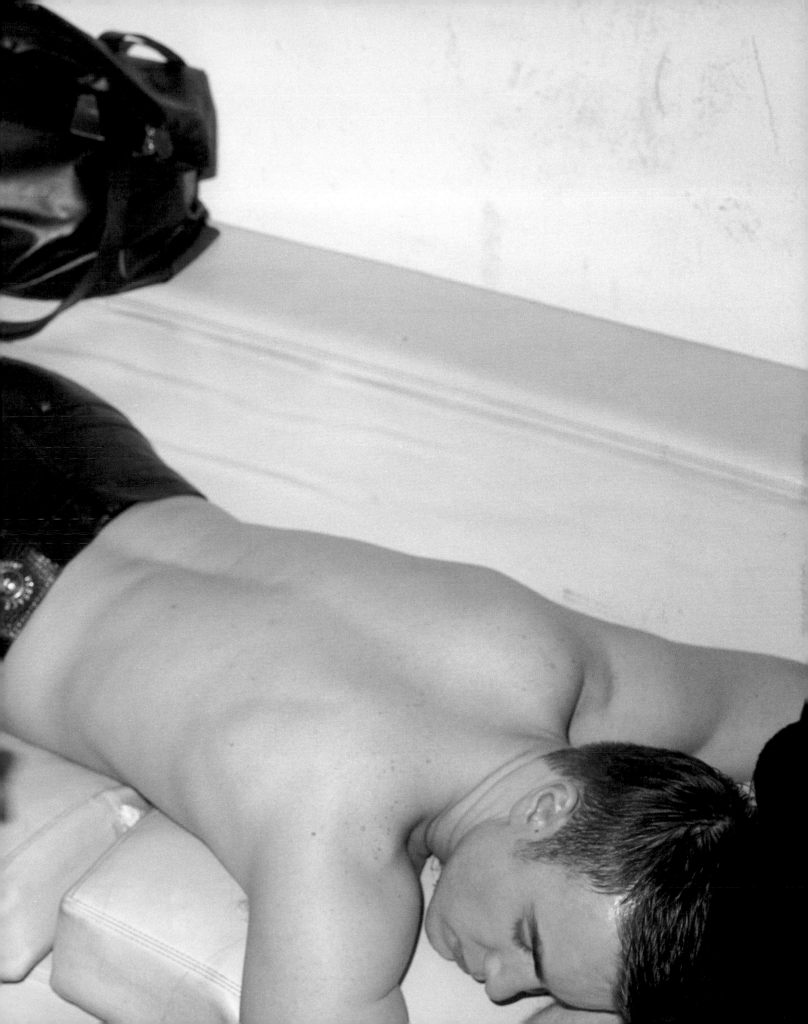

GARY ——————— The funny thing is that while we were in Take That together, me and Robbie actually got on very well. There was never a reason for us not to get on. He was always so easy to work with. Obviously the feelings that were underneath it all came out later, but I always felt like we got on great. Everyone developed as singers in the band as we progressed, but Robbie came with his voice right from the start. I always enjoyed our dynamic.

MARK ——————— None of us had any idea how big 'Back for Good' would turn out to be for us. I was meant to sing it initially. I'd had one of those phone calls from Gary saying he had a song for me. I went to his house in Cheshire to do the lead vocal but it just didn't work out. The single and the video are still one of our best.

GARYGARY———————— The single before 'Back for Good' was 'Sure', which had been a number one, and everyone was very worried that it was too much of a change to go from that to the sound of 'Back for Good'. 'Sure' was what you would've called New Jack Swing at the time. It was the R. Kelly sound that was massive everywhere, so we weren't completely convinced we were going with the right song for the follow-up. The first sign of it being big was when we were asked to perform it on the *Brits*. Nigel had said to the producers of the show, 'They'll only perform if they do their new single' and they'd said absolutely not. Everyone either does a duet or a single they're being nominated for.

Nigel left the single with them, saying, 'When you want Take That on your show, that's what they'll be singing.' We thought he'd lost it. The next day the producers phoned back and said we could do it. The day after the performance we got A-listed at every single radio station in the country and had to pull the release date of the song forward. It was an out-of-the-box smash hit for us – by far the biggest selling single we had first time round. We didn't feel any change of perception with us at the time, though. It was just a big hit record. But on reflection you can look back and see how important that song was for what Take That were. There were so many boy bands at the time that were absolutely world class.

NSync and Backstreet Boys were flying in from America. And this was our perfect deterrent to them all. It seemed to lift us up out of the competition.

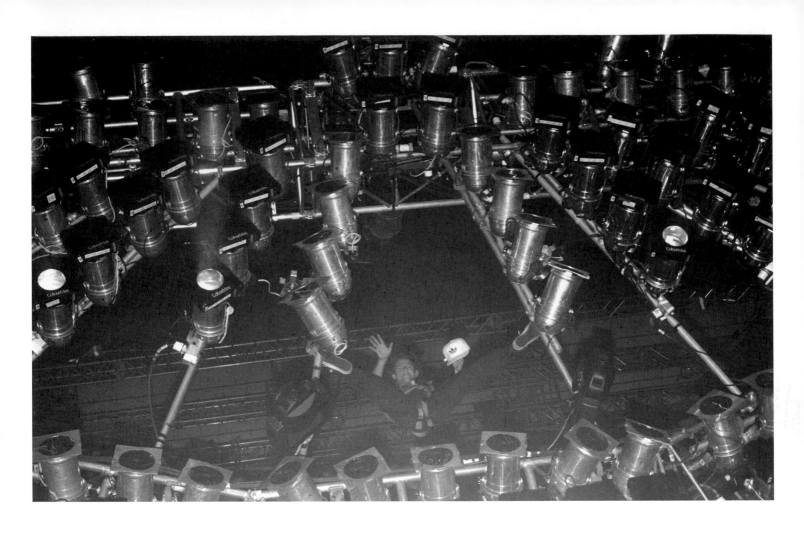

MARK ——————— The football games between me and Rob were always
a highlight backstage before we went on for a show.
We were once in a hotel in Belgium and we'd just
finished a show and we all went into the dining room and
trashed it with a game of football. Nigel bollocked us
once the bill came in.

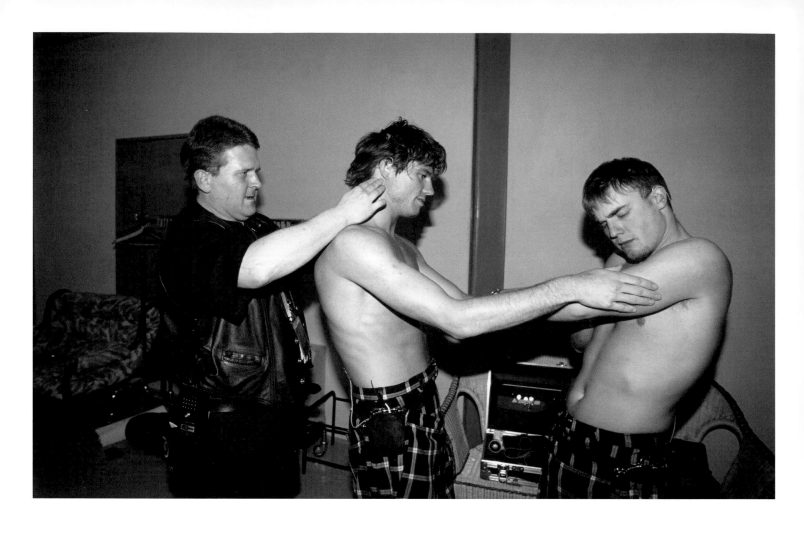

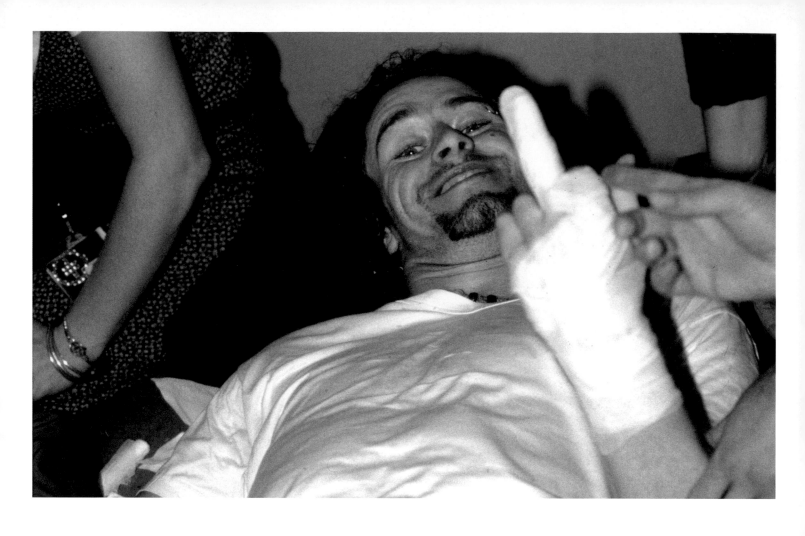

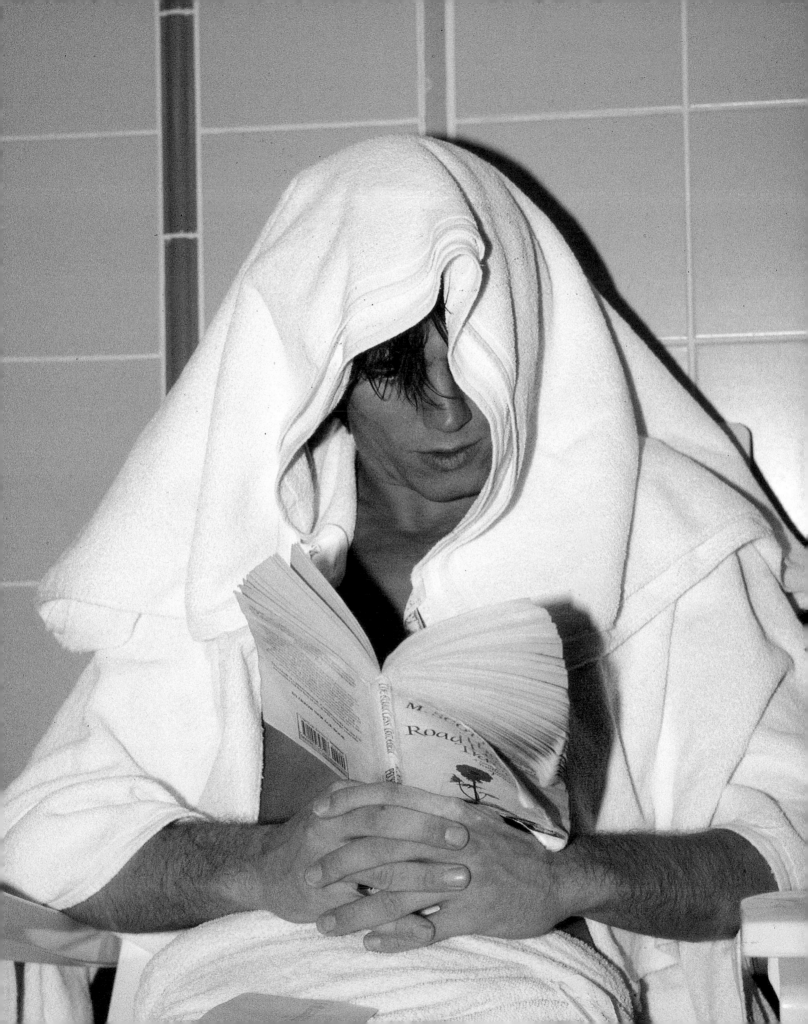

MARK —————— I'd like a copy of this picture. I don't have any memorabilia up around the house from the first time around, but I'd like this. The only way I can describe how it felt in these moments is by likening it to a football team playing in the FA Cup Final. You've just scored the winning goal and your teammate, who you've trained with for years, is the first one to tackle you to the floor. A real glory moment. It was great to share this with my best mate.

JASON ——————— We had mini-me's on tour to do 'It Only Takes a Minute' with us. I did the choreography with them.

HOWARD ——————— I met my mini-me again, not long ago. I was DJ'ing and a guy came up to the DJ booth and asked to speak to me. I told him to wait a minute while I was mixing a record and then I went over to have a chat and he said, 'I was you on tour once.' It absolutely floored me. But we had a good laugh about it.

JASON ——————— For the time on the road your family are the caterers, musicians, truck drivers, riggers, sound guys, dancers and everyone involved in making it happen. A lot of these guys are still with us now, which makes me really proud. People will leave other tours to do ours. I've heard it's known in the industry to be one of the nicest tours to do, which couldn't make me happier. It sounds corny, but there's a lot of smiling on our tours. It's always been a well-oiled machine, but you like to think it's a bit of a pyramid system where you let the good humour go down from the top, so to speak. You hear of tours that are nightmares for the crew, and I couldn't stand it if people thought going on tour with Take That was like that.

MARK ——————— The tour buses became a little diary of everything that happened while we were away. You could clock every little town we'd been to and quite a few of the people we'd met through the graffiti on them. I must say the drivers were always very forgiving about it.

HOWARD —————— Rob asleep in an airport lounge and Jay doing
exercises was quite a frequent scenario.

HOWARD ———————— You never really get used to situations like this.
The amount of time and energy that people put into
being fans takes your breath away. It's funny the
difference between female fans and what men will
do. When I've been DJ'ing I've seen guys standing
at the front of the DJ booth raising their hands. But
it's nothing like what women will do when they're
a fan of something. The passion doesn't compare.

JASON ———————— It could be a band meeting today apart from the
fact that Rob's there. Gary spinning his JD and Coke
round in his hand and holding court in a Versace vest,
which we all thought was the thing to wear at the
time. We call our meetings BBMs (Big Band Meetings)
or LBMs (Little Band Meetings). An LBM was about
what we were going to eat after a show. And a BBM
would be 'Rob's going to leave the band'.

GARY ———————— If I'm honest, a lot of the conversations from this
tour were about the girls from the night before. We
had a lot of boyish fun back then. I watch the show
Entourage now and it's not far off what we used to
get up to. We were certainly living the pop-star life.

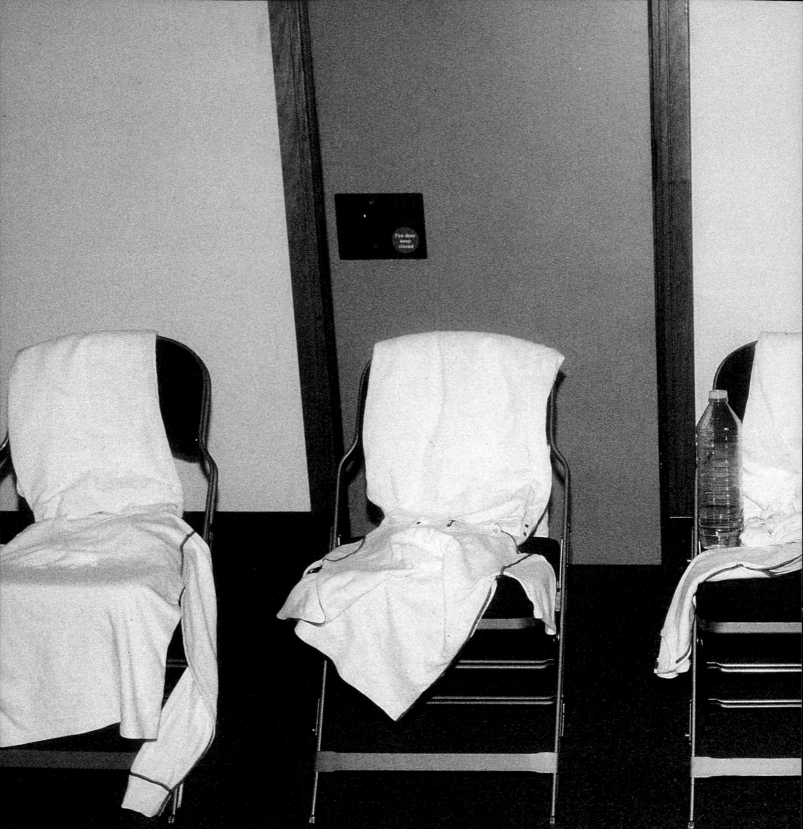

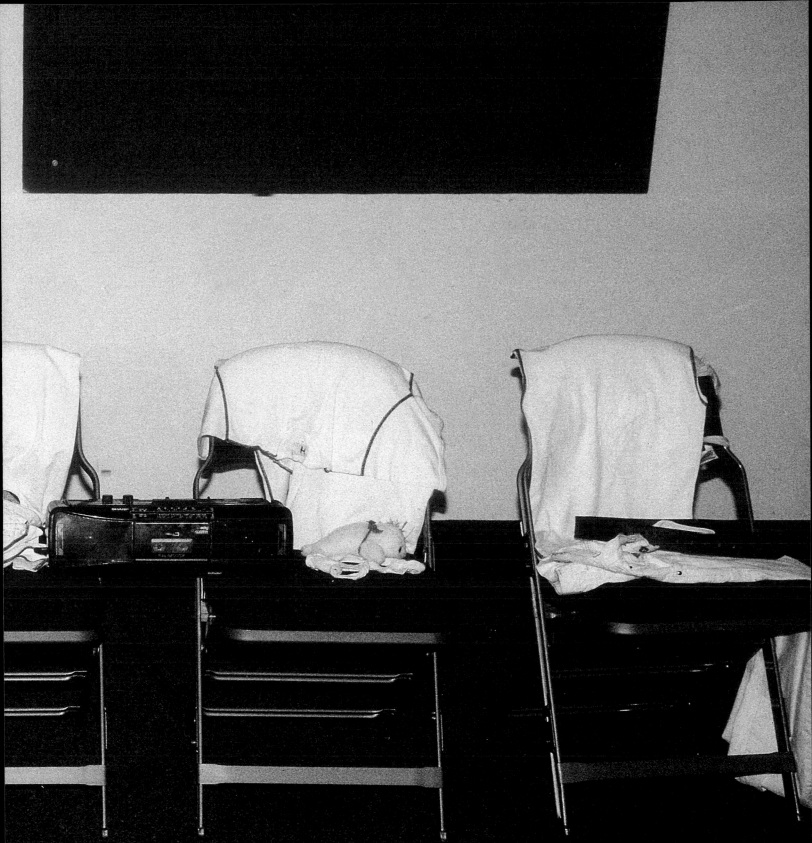

HOWARD ——————— I cried after Rob left. It was a very worrying time for me, and I'd read the papers every day. The first time I saw the footage of the five of us together in the 'Never Forget' video after he'd left, I felt such a mixture of emotions. There was a lot of fear about what was going to happen to me as the band was coming to its end. I knew that Rob always had a good heart and I knew that he wanted to go a different way and he was right to, but it was a very sad time for me. At the same time, I was proud of what happened with 'Never Forget'. I'm proud that I sang lead vocals on a song that's probably in the top five of all the songs Take That have ever done. Personally I'd say the others are 'Patience', 'Back for Good', 'A Million Love Songs' and 'Rule the World'.

JASON ——————— Andy Coulson had always championed us in the *Sun*. I remember him very fondly. He was always very kind to us on his page.

GARY —————— Jay and Mark rehearsed the Nirvana song 'Smells Like Teen Spirit' heavily for the last tour of Take That, stage one. It was supposed to be Robbie's moment, but he'd gone and we had to do it without him. He'd wanted to be a rock star so much and that was the song he'd picked for himself. When he left we panicked but went through with it and I think we just managed to pull it off.

MARK —————— We rehearsed three rock songs for the last tour while Rob was off at Glastonbury. We did 'Rocks' by Primal Scream, 'Smells Like Teen Spirit' and Pink Floyd's 'Another Brick In The Wall'. 'Teen Spirit' was Rob's choice. We knew exactly what Rob wanted to do and who he wanted to be and it was about giving him our full support to do that thing in the band. And then he left after he got back from Glastonbury.

MARK _____ Apart from Robbie leaving, the thing I remember most about these rehearsals was that it was a really hot, beautiful summer and we were holed up in the Territorial Army grounds in Stockport. There was always a feeling that Rob was still going to turn up. The oddest thing was not him leaving on the Friday, it was him not turning up on the Monday and never coming back again.

MARK ———————— The visuals of the band have always been important to me. It's such a privilege to have had the opportunity to learn about what happens with photography and directing by being so close to it. There aren't many jobs you do that give you as much of an insight into all these different areas of the creative world that ours has. Those opportunities don't come along for everyone.

HOWARD ———————— It's just Mark all over. Paying attention to all the details, very hands-on. All that attention has served him very well for this time round.

GARK————— The '95 tour was the first time we had the money to get a lot of production on stage with us. Kim Gavin did a brilliant job. He got moving stuff on stage with us. It was the start of our really ambitious productions and it was a big step for us. There was money around us for the first time ever. We kept a lot of the props and machinery in storage afterwards. During the years we weren't together one of the only things we had to talk about between the four of us was what we were going to do with the stuff in storage. We sold most of it on. It wasn't a big deal, but it kept us in occasional contact with each other, which was always lovely.

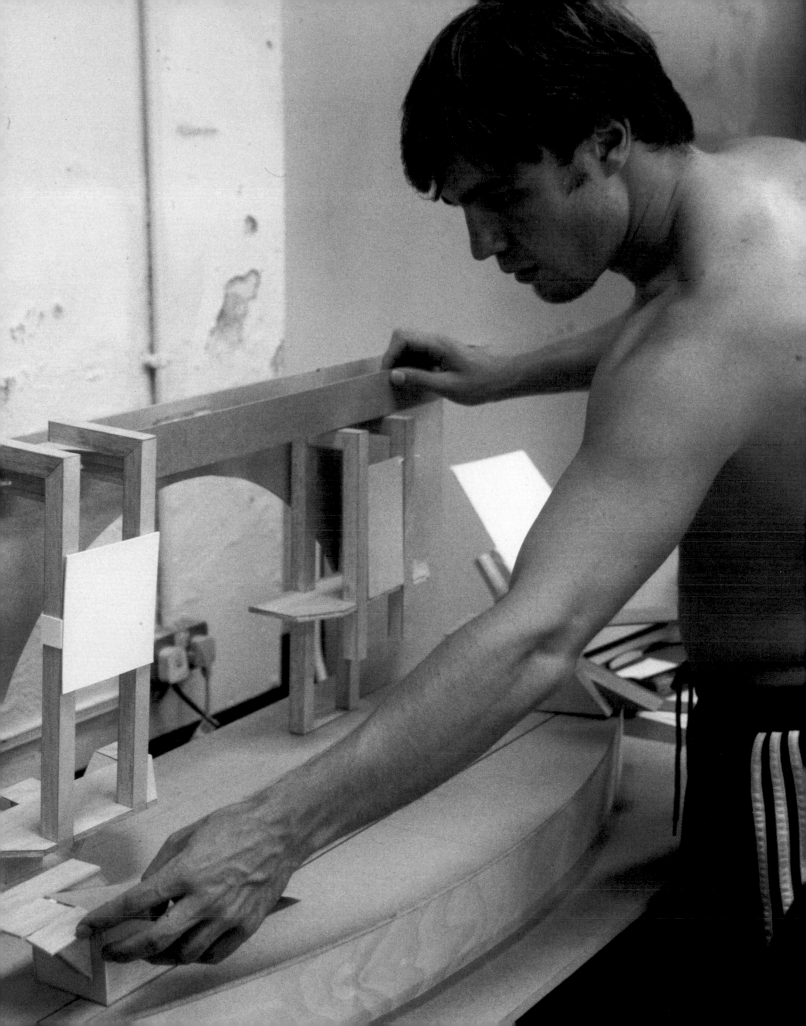

MARK _____ The live show has always been and will always be the thing at the centre of Take That. There was a real buzz backstage, and our team was lovely. Helping me to get ready is James, our security guard. He's still with us now, and so is Linda (far right). It was important when we came back to get together as many of the old team as possible. A kind of security blanket I guess.

JASON _____ Our PA, Ying, was helping me to put on my horns. She went on to be PA for the Spice Girls. She was our favourite person to be around. When Nigel couldn't come on tour with us, she'd take his place (and we always secretly hoped it'd be her). She cared about us a lot. She came to the most recent Wembley show and said everything you'd want to hear. She's just got a gift for it. She's a beautiful person.

HOWARD _____ Jenny, who's getting an eyeful of me here, used to cut my hair. We'd go round to her house and get a haircut, and then she graduated to becoming a dresser for us. She was a lovely lady.

GARY————————— The tour that Robbie had left before was the only time being in Take That felt like a job to me. We were a bit relieved Rob had gone because by that point he was doing our heads in. We'd sold all the tickets for the tour and cancelling was not an option. We've never cancelled anything to this day. It was something we had to do. Rob's gone, the job's got to be done, let's re-do it as four. Our Tour Director Kim Gavin, who really is the fifth/sixth member of Take That and who is still with us now, took over and redesigned the whole thing. Rob had all the time in the world to think how badly done by it all he'd been, but we just got on with it. We had to. When we came back for stage two, a lot of promoters said we couldn't sell tickets without Robbie. That was the feedback.

We were always of the frame of mind, 'Can we do it as a four?' and it was Jason who pointed out, 'Actually, we've done it before. And it can work.' That was probably our least favourite tour but the most important, ultimately, to us coming back all these years later.

MARK ——————— Traditionally 'Relight My Fire' has always been a closing song for us, but for this tour we'd chosen to open with it. It was the longest entrance in history: twelve minutes. It would've been even longer if Rob hadn't left just before the tour started. Bonnie was a fantastic stylist. She was great at picking out outfits that reflected things the fans knew about us, and that costume was supposed to reflect my pet iguana, Nirvana, which I'd talked about on the *Everything Changes* long-form video. We weren't nearly as involved in the costumes then as we are now, but Bonnie had a very good knack for playing on the idea of what Take That was.

JASON ———————— Howard could always leap twice as high as anyone else and make these beautiful, iconic shapes with his body. Legs all over the place. I've always secretly been a bit jealous of his athleticism and there's always been a competition between the two of us. It's healthy and friendly. But it's there.

JASON —————— There is no way that I'd get this high up on a wire now. The 'Relight My Fire' get-up wasn't very comfy, either. Our tour stylist Bonnie Brygg did the outfit. She was a bit of a replacement mother figure for us all. She'd been quite a famous ballet dancer as a young girl so she was always good with words of wisdom.

MARK _____ Some pictures just sum up perfectly what it was to be in Take That in the 90s for me. Chaos, in and out of hotels, frantic grabbing of clothes; by the time you've got to the end of it, you were battered. It was very exciting. Apart from in Paris. That's the only place it never happened. They never really got us in France.

GARY —————— Our security guards, James and Paul, have been with us through all the madness. They're still with us now. Even now this sort of thing happens. It's a very funny feeling you get from it, no mistake. It's over in a flash but its odd while it lasts.

GARY —————— The Australian tour was really odd. Rob had just left. We'd just played ten sell-out nights at Earl's Court and ten sell-out nights at the Nynex in Manchester and got to Aussie and we went on stage in Adelaide to 200 kids in a 10,000-seater arena. It wasn't the best start. We did improve, and by the time we got to Sydney it was 4,000 in 8,000-seaters, but that tour was not good for morale. So a lot of sunbathing was going on in between. Obviously me and Howard invented the Beckham pose.

HOWARD —————— Gary had just met Dawn and he was in great shape. He'd known her many years before the band even. Then she'd done a tour with us as a dancer and they'd got together. There's something about Gary that was always meant to be married. He's got a lovely home life. It looks so great from the outside and I believe that it's very happy on the inside, too. Dawn's a great girl. We're all very close to her, and their kids are smashing.

JASON —————— As Gary was preparing for his solo career he started getting a bit more chiselled. I didn't sense it at the time but, looking back, you can see him preparing himself for it physically. There was a little tension in the air towards the end about it, and Rob going was the chink in the armour. We all knew it was going to come to an end after that. And I think we were all, except for Howard, ready for it in our own ways. I was relieved, certainly. I thought, 'I can get on with my life now.'

GARG——————— The shopping bags tell quite a story. I asked Mark to take me shopping so I had some nice clothes to wear when I met Dawn. It was only two weeks into us getting together. Me and Dawn got together on the '95 tour. We finished the British leg and had to go off and tour Asia and it was killing me being apart from her. She was going to come out for five days in the middle of the tour and that was during dates we were playing in Singapore and Bangkok. I was besotted straight away.

JASON ——————— A Danish girl gave me my ring when we were on promotion. It said, 'Veni, Vidi, Vici': 'We Came, We Saw, We Conquered'. She's probably married now with seven kids, but we were close for a while.

MARK ——————— The singles chart meant so much to us. When I was growing up it mattered in my family. We'd all sit round the radio and listen to it. *The Charts* on Sunday and *Top of the Pops* on Thursday were my musical education. When our first single 'Do What You Like' came out, we were all round at Nigel's house listening to hear where we'd gone in at. When they got to number two on the countdown we genuinely thought we might be going in at number one. Of course it had gone in at number eighty-two or something. But we had no idea because we were so naive.

GARY   We sang 'Back for Good' on *Good Morning America* which was number six in the American charts at the time. We were being brought in on the tail of it already being a big hit record in America. The following evening we did *The David Letterman Show*. It was a great moment, but Robbie leaving just before overshadowed it all a bit. We were touring Australia and kept hearing the chart position in America as it was climbing, but the excitement had faded because it wasn't all of us enjoying it together. You'd hear reports back from Britain saying Rob had been on *The Big Breakfast* and when he'd been asked about Take That's American success, he'd said, 'Can they just send me the cheque in the post?' It was a bit of a mess. Not at all how we wanted to finish up. We always said we'd quit when we were on top.

GARE——————— 'Never Forget' became such a big anthem for us. It was the one that every single member of the crowd would join in with and you could see them reacting to it from the moment it started. The Queen claps in the final choruses felt like we were finally getting to master that moment in a stage show where you know it will be electrifying. Just as we were splitting up... Watching a massive audience doing those claps always looked amazing from where we were standing on the stage. I'm sure we got as much pleasure watching the audience do it as they did from the performance. Everyone knew to do the move, even the guys who had been dragged to the gigs by their wives or girlfriends. It was always a brilliant moment in the show.

MARK ——————— I was reading *The Tibetan Book of Living and Dying* on my travels. I disappeared from the hotel and walked down to the beach for a quiet half hour to myself...

HOWARD ——————— A girl had given me a bra by the pool and I invited her over for a cup of tea and it sparked off a lot of press speculation. There was a set of pictures of me and this stranger that ran in the newspapers for a while. Jason and his brother were also in the shot but the papers picked up on me and this girl and tried to say we were romantically linked. It was all nonsense.

JASON ——————— The signing sessions still go on to this day. Every time we got to a gig we put by half an hour allocated for one, just to make sure all the venue's staff and management are looked after. I couldn't begin to think how many autographs I've done in my lifetime. I've never understood the significance of them. Kids used to come into school with a famous footballer's autograph when I was growing up and everyone would gather round. I thought it was odd back then. And I was only thirteen.

MARK ——————— At the start of the band only Rob smoked. By the end we all did. I used to cut my own fringe at this time. I didn't need to, I just did.

HOWARD ——————— If Mark's looking rough then you can be guaranteed that he'd snuck off with Rob the night before to go partying. They'd sneak past security, not thinking we knew and have a night out.

MARK —————— The problem with all the travelling was that quite often
we'd only get to see the inside of hotel rooms. I did
try and get out a bit more towards the end, especially in
the Far East because I was so interested in the culture.
I guess Take That felt like college for me. It gave me
a chance to find out about music, but it also gave me
a chance to find out about life and relationships and
growing old. I'd started asking bigger questions.

GARY_____ My favourite thing is popcorn. Whenever we went
to the cinema there was a fight not to sit next to me
because I'd munch all the way through the film with
everyone else going 'shut up'.

JASON ——————— We'd all been invited to visit Gianni Versace at his house and then went to the shop. He gave us a leather jacket, a leather belt and a pair of leather gloves each and I was never out of them, and nor was Gary. You'd never felt leather like it. Like butter.

GARY —————— The press conference to announce that we were splitting up was a weird one. The person to the very left of the shot with a pair of white trainers on is David Joseph, who's now our boss. He was the junior press officer at the label at the time. There's a guy in a red and black shirt who went on to head up MTV. The whole thing was a bit of a relief to us, to be honest. I was quite excited. I knew I wanted to go on and do another record solo. We were all weighed down a little bit by the Robbie business and so it wasn't like leaving the band, it was like leaving all that endless press speculation about whether he'd come back or not behind. It felt like all the baggage of being in Take That had gone.

I drove to the press conference in my own car from my house in Cheshire and then drove back afterwards to Dawn. I put the news on and there was Moira Stewart talking about us splitting up. It was being pumped live on MTV and Radio One and I just sat on my couch thinking, 'Did we just cause all that fuss?' It was bizarre. Dawn said the same thing. She said, 'Wow. All that fuss. Just for you lot.'

MARK ——————— I drove down to the Hilton at Manchester airport from my flat in Manchester and there were four bottles of champagne waiting for us in a room upstairs. Gaz said 'Listen, lads, if anyone wants to change their mind, now's the time to do it.' And we all laughed. We'd achieved everything we could have achieved and there was nothing more left for us to do. Right at the beginning I can remember us sitting in the BHS café eating our sandwiches and saying that we should never overstay our welcome. I don't think we ever did.

HOWARD ——————— The difficulty for me was not knowing where I was going or what I was going to do afterwards. And knowing that other people, well, Gary, knew where he was going next. There was quite a bit of talk going on that we didn't know about between the record label and Gary. There was nothing untoward happening and it was probably the fair way to do it. There was a little bit of relief there for me but there was a lot of fear, too. It took me at least three or four years to get over the idea that our schedule had come to a standstill. If someone had told me on that day we would be coming back nearly ten years later, I wouldn't have believed them. What happened the second time round has just astonished me. And it would've astonished the person sitting at that press conference.

MARK ——————— I love the fact we were killed off in our last video. I thought it was quite funny that we were all thrown off a cliff. It wasn't the most comfortable of video shoots though. In fact, it was pretty miserable.

GARks;————————— We sang 'How Deep Is Your Love' on our last ever TV show in Holland. At the rehearsals we were so bored we dropped our trousers to keep us entertained. It was way before YouTube and you really didn't think for a second that any of this stuff would be seen again.

MARK ————————— Amsterdam felt like the perfect place for it to end.
I think it was the first territory we had visited outside
the UK when we started. I do remember it being an
emotional day. It was all quite surreal. Too much
smoke. The weirdest thing about it all coming to an
end was coming home. We got off the plane and into
our own cars and just drove off. A little hug and that
was that.

HOWARD ————————— On the day you didn't even register that this was the
last performance. I wasn't ready for the end, at all.
It was when we got back to Manchester airport that
it really hit home and I crashed down to earth with
a bang.

Livingstone's Illustrated Blind

Country through Libraries

TAKE ONE / INDEX

Location   Photography

Cover photograph by Phillippe McClelland
Commentary transcribed by Paul Flynn
Book design and direction by Studio Fury
in association with Jonathan Wild, 10 Management
Take That would like to thank all contributing photographers